# Dogs

Level 1 – Pink

# Helpful Hints for Reading at Home

The graphemes (written letters) and phonemes (units of sound) used throughout this series are aligned with Letters and Sounds. This offers a consistent approach to learning, whether reading at home or in the classroom.

**HERE IS A LIST OF NEW PHONEMES FOR THIS PHASE OF LEARNING. AN EXAMPLE OF THE PRONUNCIATION CAN BE FOUND IN BRACKETS.**

| Phase 2 | | | |
|---|---|---|---|
| s (sat) | a (cat) | t (tap) | p (tap) |
| i (pin) | n (net) | m (man) | d (dog) |
| g (got) | o (sock) | c (cat) | k (kin) |
| ck (sack) | e (elf) | u (up) | r (rabbit) |
| h (hut) | b (ball) | f (fish) | ff (off) |
| l (lip) | ll (ball) | ss (hiss) | |

**HERE ARE SOME WORDS WHICH YOUR CHILD MAY FIND TRICKY.**

| Phase 2 Tricky Words | | | |
|---|---|---|---|
| the | to | I | no |
| go | into | | |

## TOP TIPS FOR HELPING YOUR CHILD TO READ:

- Allow children time to break down unfamiliar words into units of sound and then encourage children to string these sounds together to create the word.

- Encourage your child to point out any focus phonics when they are used.

- Read through the book more than once to grow confidence.

- Ask simple questions about the text to assess understanding.

- Encourage children to use illustrations as prompts.

This book focuses on /d/, /g/, /o/ and /c/ and is a Pink level 1 book band.

# Can you say this sound and draw it with your finger?

It is a dog.

Sip, sip, sip.

I can pat a dog.

Pat, pat, pat.

Run to get it.

# The dog has got it.

# A dog is fun.

I can hug the dog.

©2023 **BookLife Publishing Ltd.**
King's Lynn, Norfolk, PE30 4LS, UK
ISBN 978-1-80505-084-1

All rights reserved. Printed in China.
A catalogue record for this book is available from the British Library.

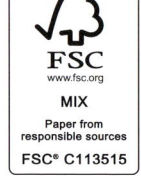

**Dogs**
Written by William Anthony
Designed by Lucy Otter

# An Introduction to BookLife Readers...

Our Readers have been specifically created in line with the London Institute of Education's approach to book banding and are phonetically decodable and ordered to support each phase of the Letters and Sounds document.

Each book has been created to provide the best possible reading and learning experience. Our aim is to share our love of books with children, providing both emerging readers and prolific page-turners with beautiful books that are guaranteed to provoke interest and learning, regardless of ability.

**BOOK BAND GRADED** using the Institute of Education's approach to levelling.

**PHONETICALLY DECODABLE** supporting each phase of Letters and Sounds.

**EXERCISES AND QUESTIONS** to offer reinforcement and to ascertain comprehension.

**CLEAR DESIGN** to inspire and provoke engagement, providing the reader with clear visual representations of each non-fiction topic.

**AUTHOR INSIGHT:**
**WILLIAM ANTHONY**

William Anthony's involvement with children's education is quite extensive. He has written over 60 titles with BookLife Publishing so far, across a wide range of subjects. William graduated from Cardiff University with a 1st Class BA (Hons) in Journalism, Media and Culture, creating an app and a TV series, among other things, during his time there.

William Anthony has also produced work for the Prince's Trust, a charity that helps young people with their professional future. He has created animated videos for a children's education company that works closely with the charity.

This book focuses on /d/, /g/, /o/ and /c/ and is a Pink level 1 book band.

**Image Credits** Images are courtesy of Shutterstock.com. With thanks to Getty Images, Thinkstock Photo and iStockphoto. Cover – azure1, Brovko Serhii, Robert Bodnar T, smrm1977. 4–5 – MaraZe, Tara Lynn and Co. 6–7 – Eric Isselee, Ermolaev Alexander. 8–9 – Ksenia Raykova. 10–11 – ANURAK PONGPATIMET, Martin Valigursky.

# BookLife Non-Fiction Readers

**EXPLORE A WORLD OF NON-FICTION WITH OUR DECODABLE READER RANGE**

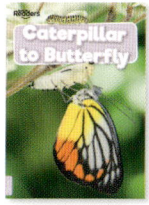 Caterpillar to Butterfly — 9781839278938

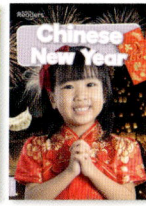 Chinese New Year — 9781839278921

 Dig a Pit — 9781839278945

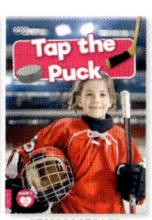 Tap the Puck — 9781839278952

 Pets — 9781839278976

 Picnic — 9781839278969

 Queens and Kings — 9781839278990

 Vets — 9781839278983

 At the Fun Fair — 9781839279010

 Look Up! — 9781839279003

 At the Shop — 9781839279027

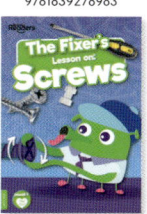 The Fixer's Lesson on Screws — 9781839279034

 Stay Safe Online — 9781839279058

 Habitats — 9781839279041

**MORE COMING SOON**

# BookLife PUBLISHING

The BookLife Readers begin with the very basics of **phonetically decodable reading**. Starting with the earliest step of **CVC** words–words comprising of a consonant, a vowel and a consonant–and building on this combination slowly, the reader follows a prescribed format taken directly from the recognised **Letters and Sounds** educational document.

By aligning our books with Letters and Sounds, we offer our readers a consistent approach to learning, whether at home or in the classroom. Our Readers each feature a focus sound to help learners practice reading specific graphemes. These focus sounds will feature more heavily in that title than in others in the same band. The illustrations and photographs guide the reader, helping to deliver reading progression through the scheme in a colourful and exciting way. As a reader moves through the book band levels, the page numbers, levels of repetition and sentence structure complexity all advance at a rate which encourages development without halting enjoyment.

To find out more about this exciting reading scheme, visit **www.booklife.co.uk**